THE CONTRIBUTION OF EARLY TRAVEL NARRATIVES TO THE HISTORICAL GEOGRAPHY OF GREECE

THE TWENTY-SECOND

J.L. MYRES MEMORIAL LECTURE

THE CONTRIBUTION OF EARLY TRAVEL NARRATIVES TO THE HISTORICAL GEOGRAPHY OF GREECE

A Lecture delivered at
New College, Oxford, on 6th May, 2003

by

MALCOLM WAGSTAFF

University of Oxford

Published in 2004 by
The University of Oxford

ISBN 0–9546647–0–1

Typeset by Cambrian Typesetters, Frimley, Surrey
and printed by Halstan & Co. Ltd., Amersham, Bucks

THE CONTRIBUTION OF EARLY TRAVEL NARRATIVES TO THE HISTORICAL GEOGRAPHY OF GREECE

I was completely surprised by the invitation to deliver this lecture. But I was also honoured to be asked to join such a distinguished list of lecturers, some of whom I have been privileged to know. I was delighted as well. Strangely, my own career and that of John Myres have touched at various points, though − of course − chronologically very separate. I should like to start, then, with some comments on this historical contingency, progress to the attractions of early travel narratives for scholars, including geographers, then outline what information historical geographers can find in them and conclude with an examination of some of the methodological problems involved in using travel narratives as historical sources.

First, then some remarks on the historical contingency of relationship. Myres was the first Gladstone Professor of Greek and Lecturer in Ancient Geography in the University of Liverpool (1907–10)[1], my University. He was also related to P.M. Roxby (1880–1947), first head of the University's newly created (1909) Department of Geography[2]. Myres and I both went to Greece as under-graduates, a difference of a mere 69 years intervening, and that experience changed our lives. Both of us had early interests in Crete. In due course, my developing interest in the historical geography of Greece was fed by Myres' collection of papers, *Geographical History in Greek Lands* (1953), and it was one of the very first books on Greece that I bought.

Our contacts continued even to Southampton. Myres became involved in intelligence work and privateering in Greece during the First World War, at first in a rather casual way and then with a commission in the RNVR[3]. In May 1917 an Australian classicist, Lt. O.H.T. Rishbeth, RNVR (1886–1942), joined the Admiralty Intelligence Department and was posted to the Aegean. As a student at Merton College (1911–14), Rishbeth may have attended lectures by the Wykeham Professor of Ancient History. Like Myres, he had a distinguished war career and was gazetted Chevalier in the Greek Order of the Redeemer in 1918. Also like Myres, he seems to have been involved in operations in and around the Dodecanese. This is suggested, first, by Rishbeth's choice of a paper to give to a session on 'Some Problems of Political Geography' organised by Section E of the British Association for the Advancement of Science in September 1919; it was on the Dodecanese. Secondly, with Eleftherios Venizelos (the former Prime Minister of Greece), Rishbeth was one

---

1 T.J. Dunbabin, 'Sir John Myres, 1869–1954', *Proceedings of the British Academy*, 41 (1955), 349–365

2 R.W. Steel, 'Geography at the University of Liverpool', In: R.W. Steel and R. Lawton (eds.), *Liverpool Essays in Geography: A Jubilee Collection*, London: Longmans 1967, 1–23

3 J.N.L. Myres, *The Tenth J.L. Myres Memorial Lecture: Commander J.L. Myres, RNVR − The Blackbeard of the Aegean*, London: Leopard's Head Press 1980.

of the four people invited to respond to Myres' lecture on the same topic to the Royal Geographical Society in March of the following year[4]. In 1922, Rishbeth joined the then University College of Southampton and became its first Professor of Geography four years later[5]. Rishbeth's last and sadly unpublished paper was on the corn supply of ancient Greece, a subject which would surely have appealed to Myres.

With these historical contingencies out of the way, we can turn to early travel narratives and their contribution to the historical geography of Greece. On the face of it, this does not seem to have been a topic in which Myres was particularly interested. The select list of his publications at the end of *Geographical History in Greek Lands* suggests as much. However, in his lecture on *The Value of Ancient History* given in Oxford in 1910, Myres claimed to have read travel works whilst preparing himself for 'Greats', and told his listeners that they would understand the 'queerness' (we would perhaps now say the 'otherness') of ancient Greek civilisation only through travel: 'Go, in travel-books if not in steamers, to the modern East, or even to the remoter parts of the Mediterranean'[6]. Furthermore, Myres' association with Naval Intelligence in the Second World War may have turned his attention back to travel narratives[7]. He was largely responsible for the Geographical Handbook on the Dodecanese, under Italian occupation since 1912, and is credited with a hand in others in the same series. The introduction to the third volume of the Geographical Handbook on Greece, *Regional Geography*, mentions that the compilers had used 'the earlier modern accounts of travel in Greece', notably those of Colonel Leake, for they 'included careful topographical descriptions in their texts'. Indeed, echoes of travel narratives can be heard throughout the volume, while two of Leake's descriptions are quoted in Volume One, *Physical Geography, History, Administration and Peoples*[8]. I submit, then, that my topic is entirely appropriate to a lecture commemorating John Myres.

At this point, I need to define what I mean by travel narratives. In the context of this lecture, travel narratives are the accounts of journeys written and – importantly – published by travellers of west European origin who visited Greece in the 'long' eighteenth century. There were earlier travellers, to be sure, and some Muslims[9], but I am particularly interested in the period between the Venetian

---

4 Public Record Office (PRO): Adm 377/123.266; *Merton College Register 1911*, 87–88; *Report of the British Association for the Advancement of Science, Transactions of Section E, Bournemouth 9–13 September, 1919*, 225–226; J.L. Myres, 'The Dodecanese', *Geographical Journal* 56 (1920), 329–47, 425–46 (441–45)

5 M. Wagstaff, *Geography: The First Seventy Years at the University of Southampton*, Southampton: Department of Geography, University of Soutampton, 1996, 11–12

6 J.L. Myres, 'The value of ancient history', In his: *Geographical History in Greek Lands*, Oxford: Clarendon Press, 1953, 34–71 (66, 68–69)

7 Dubabin, *op. cit.*, 362; W.M. Koelsch, '*John Linton Myres, 1869–1954*', Geographers Biographical Studies 16, London: Mansell, 1995, 53–62 (55); J.N.L. Myres, *op. cit.*, 11–12

8 Naval Intelligence Division, *Geographical Handbook Series: Greece*, London: 1944, Vol. 1, 47, 362; Vol. 3, 22

9 P.P. Morphopoulos, *L'Image de la Grèce chez les Voyageurs francaises (du XVIe au début au XVIIIe siècle)*, Ph.D. Thesis, John Hopkins University, Baltimore 1947; D. Constantine, *Early Greek Travellers and the Hellenic Ideal*, Cambridge: Cambridge University Press 1984

Table 1: Travel Narratives on Greece: An Analysis of *Published Travels to Greece in the Library of Henry M. Blackmer II* (Sale Catalogue, London: Sotheby's 1989)

Language (No.)	Dates of Publication				
	1600–50	1651–1700	1701–50	1751–1800	1801–30
English	4	1	4	4	29
French	1	9	3	7	17
Others	2	2	0	1	2
Total	7	12	7	12	48

Caveats
• obvious 'works of organisation' are excluded
• the publication date may be much later than the actual journey
• translations are included
• some misallocation between dates may have occurred

conquest of the Morea (1685–90) and the emergence of an independent Greek state under British, French and Russian protection (1830). The eighteenth century was seen subsequently as a golden age of travel writing, at least in English[10]. Greece at the time was no more than a geographical expression, as Metternich might have said. It did not correspond to a political state. The Greek lands were part of the Ottoman Empire, and for most eighteenth century travellers, Greece covered those places featured as Greek in the writings of Antiquity. For present purposes we can adopt a convenient definition of Greece, which corresponds with the state as it took its current form in 1947.

It is difficult and maybe impossible to know just how many people visited Greece in our period. Not all left accounts, even in manuscript form. They were probably very few, despite Hobhouse's comment in 1810 that 'Attica at present swarms with travellers'[11]; the mass influx of visitors came after Greek independence. The sale catalogue of Henry Blackmer's famous library lists 86 purely travel books published on Greece in English, French and other languages between 1600 and 1830, 67 (77.8 per cent) after 1700 (Table 1)[12]. The published travellers of the eighteenth-early nineteenth century were untypical and constituted a small sub-set of a not very large group.

Most of the travel narratives about Greece from the 'long' eighteenth century are

10 W.C. Brown, 'The popularity of English travel books about the Near East, 1775–1825', *Philological Quarterly*, 15 (1936), 70–80; F. Stark, *Riding to the Tigris*, London: John Murray, 1959, 20

11 J.C. Hobhouse, *A Journey through Albania and Other Provinces of Turkey in Europe and Asia to Constantinople during the Years 1809 and 1810*, London, 1813, Vol. 1, 302

12 *Published Travels to Greece in the Library of Henry M. Blackmer II*, London: Sotheby's 1989

prose works and retain the format of a journal. Some took the form of letters[13]. All were edited for publication and additional material was inserted at that point[14], especially quotations from the ancient authors. Many travel narratives are precise about the chronology of the journeys reported; Colonel Leake's meticulous recording of time to the hour and minute appears obsessive, but then he was dead-reckoning his travel times as an aid to future map-making[15]. Other travel writers produced a sequential account without many fixed temporal points. Together they contributed to a particular genre of literature, composed to entertain perhaps more than to instruct. However, from at least the early sixteenth century and specifically in the case of the English from 1757, when Josiah Tucker, Rector of St. Stephen's in Bristol, published his *Instructions for Travellers*, the 'good' traveller was expected to collect and publish information on social, economic and political conditions, alongside that about climate and land use[16]. Early travel narratives, then, contain varying amounts of 'serious' material. Personal comments on people, places and situations abound, along with reflections on the decay of civilisation and the sublimity of landscapes, with or without ruins. Everything was fitted into the journal format or woven into the informal fabric of the 'private' letter.

The rich material in travel narratives has attracted considerable attention over the last twenty years from a variety of scholars[17] – archaeologists, geographers, historians, and literature specialists. Their potential, however, was appreciated long ago. For example, geographical research in the early nineteenth century largely involved the careful collation of information taken from travel narratives[18]. The 1920s saw something of an upsurge in interest in travel narratives about the Near East[19], perhaps stimulated by the League of Nations' mandates in the region, the emergence of republican Turkey, and significant anniversaries in modern Greek history. Although Edward Said ignored Greece in his famous study, *Orientalism* (1978), that book has

13 Eg. G.E. Marinden (ed.), *The Letters of John B.S. Morritt of Rokeby*, London: John Murray, 1914

14 Something of the editorial process behind Hobhouse's *A Journey through Albania . . .*, *op.cit.*, is revealed by Lord Byron's correspondence, L. A. Marchand (ed.), Vol. 2, *'Famous in My Time'. Byron's Letters and Journals*, London: John Murray 1973: 61 Byron to Hobhouse 23 July, 1811; 81 Byron to James Cawthorn 25 August, 1811; 109 Byron to Francis Hodgson 8 October, 1811; 113–14 Byron to Hobhouse 13 October, 1811; 125 and n.1 Byron to Hobhouse 3 November 1811; 131 Byron to Hobhouse 17 November, 1811; 135–36 Byron to Hobhouse 3 December, 1811

15 W.M. Leake, *Travels in the Morea*, London 1830; *Travels in Northern Greece*, London, 1835

16 J.R. Hale (ed.), *The Travel Journal of Antonio de Beatis. Germany, Switzerland, the Low Countries, France and Italy, 1517–18*, London: The Hakluyt Society, 2nd series, No. 150, 1979, 22–31; J. Howell, *Instructions for Forreine Travell [sic]] 1642, collated with the second edition of 1650, carefully edited by Edward Arber*, London: English Reprints, 1869; J. Tucker, *Instructions for Travellers*, London, 1757

17 C. Chard, *Pleasure and Guilt on the Grand Tour: Travel Writing and Imaginative Geography 1600–1820*, Manchester: Manchester University Press, 1994; J. Duncan and D. Gregory (eds.), *Writes of Passage: Reading Travel Writing*, London: Routledge, 1999

18 J.D.Overton, 'A theory of exploration', *Journal of Historical Geography*, 7 (1981), 53–70

19 Brown, *op. cit.*; F.L. Lucas, 'The literature of Greek travels', *Transactions of the Royal Society of Literature*, ns 17 (1930), 17–40

been credited with the more recent revival of general interest in travel narratives[20]. Some scholars, like Chard, became interested in the 'discourse of travel' and the rules which governed the production of a particular type of literature[21]. Some geographers, for their part, have tried to deconstruct the 'imaginative geographies' of the early travellers' world and to understand how these were created. Other geographers have been concerned with the roles of 'white imperial women travellers in the production of geographical knowledge' and in 'feminist geographies of the gaze', while seeking to develop 'colonial discourse analysis'[22]. Clearly, these scholars are attracted by a characteristic of travel narratives identified by Ernest and Merrens in a paper published, like *Orientalism*, in 1978:

> 'What travel accounts do tell us a lot about, what they provide valid evidence of, is the qualities of those who produced the accounts. They are, that is to say, valid as evidence of their authors' values, opinions and writing skills. As representations of the scene the traveller saw (as well as the scene he either did not see or saw but chose not to report on), they are neither more nor less selective and imaginative renderings'[23].

Yet, it is precisely the representational material in travel narratives which Myres' academic descendants now working on the archaeology, history and historical geography of Greece wish to exploit. Following the pioneering work of the Minnesota Messenia Expedition (1972), all the published regional archaeological surveys in Greece have made use of travel narratives in reconstructing the historical geographies of their study areas[24], bringing the time-frame forwards and shedding light on pre-modern or traditional socio-economic systems. Among historians, Helen Angelomatis-Tsougarakis has attempted 'to give a comprehensive account of the British travellers' perceptions of early nineteenth century Greece (1800–21), and compare these with the evidence of travellers of other nationalities, the Greek sources, and other modern historical works'[25]. Her survey covers what she calls physical and comparative geography (including settlement, population, communications and migration), land tenure, taxation, currency circulation, prices and wages, commerce, manufacturing and stock rearing. Helen's book is perhaps the nearest we get at the moment to an historical geography of Greece at the end of the 'long' eighteenth century.

20 S. Faroqui, *Approaching Ottoman History: An Introduction to the Sources*, Cambridge: Cambridge University Press 1999, 110

21 Chard, *op. cit.*, 12–14

22 Blunt and Wells, *op. cit.*, 116–17, 119, 182–87

23 J.E. Ernst and H.R. Merrens, 'Praxis and theory in the writing of American historical geography', *Journal of Historical Geography*, 4 (1978), 277–90

24 W.A. McDonald and G.R. Rapp (eds.), *The Minnesota Messenia Expedition: Reconstructing a Bronze Age Regional Environment*, Minneapolis: University of Minnesota Press, 1972

25 H. Angelomatis-Tsougarakis, *The Eve of the Greek Revival: British Travellers' Perceptions of Early Nineteenth-Century Greece*, London: Routledge 1990, xv

What do we mean by historical geography? Myres himself defined Geography in various but related ways characteristic of his time. In 'Ancient Geography in Modern Education' he wrote something to which geographers can still subscribe:

> 'In geographical science the relation of these facts [of observation] with each other is their relation in space; the geographer ascertains, records, compares, and interprets distributions, the arrangement of things on or in relation to the surface of the earth'[26].

My definition of *historical geography* would fall within this formulation of what the geographer does, but I see the sub-discipline as the study in time past of those places and topics which are of concern to geographers working on the present. Thus, I would include, for example, 'the existence, production and representation of gendered spaces'[27], at one extreme, and the location of ancient place names in the tradition of Leake, at the other, with the reconstruction of regional settlement and land-use patterns – my own particular interests – somewhere in between.

The travel narratives provide information on all these and, indeed, on other topics as well[28] (Table 2). All of them may not appear to be *Geography*, but where the information is spatially referenced, or can be made so, then the comparisons and interpretations mentioned by Myres can be made. A few examples of clearly historico-geographical material may be taken from Colonel Leake's travels.

Contemporaries reckoned that Colonel William Martin Leake (1777–1860) was, to quote Dr. William Smith, 'a first-rate observer, a good scholar, and a man of sound judgement and great sagacity'[29]. Modern scholars have echoed these sentiments[30]. Leake occasionally recorded the state of the weather and added some comments on climate. Thus, in his *Travels in Northern Greece* Leake published his largely qualitative observations on the weather at Ioannina in the summer of 1810 and commented that 'this year has hardly been an average one' and that 'there has been more rain during the winter and spring, and less hot and dry weather in the summer than usual'[31]. Elsewhere he makes brief comments on rural settlements. For example, he noted that 'few' of the villages of Mani were 'very small' (45–50 houses, on average), but that none were 'like the tjiftliks of the Turkish districts of Greece'[32]. Leake actually has much to contribute to the debate on the processes of *çiftlikisation* in Thessaly and Macedonia, that is the conversion of communities of independent farmers into

26 Myres, *Geographical History in Greek Lands, op. cit.,* 72–102 (74)

27 Blunt and Wells, *op. cit.,* 116

28 For the range of topics see R. Schiffer, *Oriental Panorama: British Travellers in 19th Century Turkey,* Amsterdam-Atlanta GA: Rodopi, 1999

29 W. Smith (ed.), *A Dictionary of Greek and Roman Geography,* London: John Murray 1873, Vol. 1, 1017

30 Eg. H. Angelomatis-Tsougarakis, *The Eve of the Greek Revival: British Travellers' Perceptions of Early Nineteenth Century Greece,* London: Routledge 1990, 20

31 W.M. Leake, *Travels in Northern Greece,* London, 1835, Vol. 4, 227–28

32 W.M. Leake, *Travels in the Morea,* London, 1830, Vol. 1, 243–44

Table 2: Topics in the Historical Geography of Greece for which Travel Narratives provide Information

Climate
- references to weather
- comparisons from year to year

Appearances of Places
- landscapes
- ancient sites
- contemporary towns (relatively few descriptions of villages)
- prominent buildings (usually urban)

Existence Location and Typology of Settlements
- *Kefalokhorio Cf. Çiftlik*
- Monastery   *Metokhi*
- *Mandhra*

Land Use and Economy
- crops and animals seen
- manufacturing
- commerce
- shipping

Population (Numbers and Composition)
- Christians/Jews/Muslims ('Turks')
- Albanians/Bulgarians/Greeks/'Turks' (*Koniadhes/Osmanlı*)
- spatial distributions

Administration
- designation and spatial pattern of administrative units (Eg. *kaza/nahiye/vilayet*)
- 'traditional' regions/*pays* (Eg. Tsakonia)
- types and level of taxation

Routes
- lines of movement (and network)
- relation to settlements and land use
- frequency of use by travellers = importance (to western travellers)
- connectivity
- harbours and ports

Materiality of Travel
- availability and condition of horses/mules
- quality of roads
- posthouses, inns, private/monastic accommodation
- *dervenis/derbents*
- risks: disease/illness, bandits/pirates/privateers

sharecroppers and day-labourers and the emergence of settlements with a distinctive built form[33]. His descriptions of ancient sites vary in length and detail, but they are numerous and cover such wide areas of Greece that he seems to have been almost everywhere. On routes, John Bennet, Jack Davies and Fariha Zarinebaf-Shahr have shown how these can be reconstructed from the data provided by travellers, in this case Leake's contemporary, William Gell, and how the reconstructions provide a greater understanding of the entire landscape through which the routes passed[34]. References to the conditions of the *hans* and descriptions of over-night accommodation in private houses (rarely satisfactory) or monasteries (often better), together with complaints about the delays in getting transport, reveal much of the materiality of actual travel and the differences experienced between routes.

Attempts to reconstruct a regional geography of, say, the Morea c.1800, after the manner of Ralph Brown's *Mirror for Americans* or Carl Sauer's *Early Spanish Main*[35], require the combination of information from several travellers. Individual travellers, even Leake, did not go everywhere. The same is true for efforts to reconstruct the pattern of land use or to describe the appearance and functions of a well-frequented town like Tripolitza or Ioannina. One account is rarely comprehensive enough on its own. Drawings and paintings made by or for the travellers should be brought in here, together with contemporary maps and plans. A surprising amount of visual material is available.

Combining visual, textual and cartographic information raises various technical problems. But there is also a larger question in synthesising material, namely the size of the time bracket from which sources should be drawn for them to be represented as broadly contemporary with one another. Too short a time period and one runs the risk of only one travel account being available, and that one possibly unsatisfactory or unreliable. Make the time bracket very wide, and one may have a lot of material but lose a degree of contemporaneity, possibly missing as well any changes which may have taken place over time. The uncertainty principle seems to apply here: precision on place may mean uncertainty about time and temporal change; relative precision on time may mean a lack of detail about place. There is, of course, a tendency amongst scholars to assume continuity between the situation described by the travellers and an earlier or later one which is undocumented. It is a particularly dangerous habit in Greece where both early and recent travellers have been impressed by the apparent continuities in society, economy, manners and built form. Myres, for example, wrote that 'a modern Cretan village is amazingly like its

33 Leake, *Travels in Northern Greece, ibid.*; B. McGowan, *Economic Life in the Ottoman Empire. Taxation, Trade and the Struggle for Land, 1600–1800*, Cambridge: Cambridge University Press, 1981

34 J. Bennet, J.L. Davis and F. Zarinebaf-Shahr, 'Sir William Gell's Itinerary in the Pylia and regional landscapes in the Morea in the Second Ottoman Period', *Hesperia*, 69 (2000), 343–380

35 R.H. Brown, *Mirror for Americans: Likeness of the Eastern Seaboard, 1810*, New York: American Geographical Society, 1943; C.O. Sauer, *The Early Spanish Main*, Berkeley and Los Angeles: University of California Press; Cambridge: Cambridge University Press, 1966

Minoan predecessor, at all points where we can compare their arrangements and economy'[36]. He would probably have attributed the similarities, at least in part, to '. . . the Mediterranean climate and the rest of the Mediterranean regime' which in his day was generally assumed to be stable and deterministic[37]. Actual continuity, however, needs to be tested, examined and explained[38].

Travel narratives contain the results of personal observation and experience. To that extent they appear to offer unmediated information. However, 'eighteenth century Englishmen [and, one could add, Frenchmen, Germans and Italians] lived in a partly make-believe classical world'[39]. Nearly everything which such travellers observed in our period was seen through the eyes of a person educated by means of the Latin and Greek classical writers, the eyes of an antiquarian and collector[40]. This explains two striking characteristics of travel writing about Greece in the 'long' eighteenth century. The first is the note of disappointment about the condition and behaviour of the contemporary Greek people; they simply failed to live up to the travellers' noble expectations. The other characteristic is the emphasis upon Antiquity, whether ancient sites or the literary and historical associations of place, to the neglect of much that might have been noted in the contemporary landscape. Nonetheless, the travellers were on a learning curve. Preparatory reading may have told them what to expect, creating 'a geography of expectation'[41], which blunted the sharpness of personal encounter and clouded judgements. However, it seems clear that two developments took place during a prolonged stay in Greece or the wider Near East. On the one hand, critical understanding improved. On the other, the once unusual and exotic became commonplace and thus less likely to be recorded. Allowance must be made for these characteristics when using travel narratives.

Travel narratives provide information which is essentially the result of sporadic observation and collection, but organised in terms of a sequential journey. Except when commenting on the ruins of empire and the degeneration of peoples, the travel books are not generally works of reflection. The lack of reflection and systematic comment can be remedied by using travel narratives in conjunction with what Ralph Brown called 'works of organisation'. Although these may be rooted in actual

36 J.L. Myres, 'Ancient geography in modern education', In: *Geographical History . . ., op.cit.,* 72–102 (88)

37 J.L. Myres 'The causes of rise and fall in the population of the ancient world', In: *Geographical History . . ., op. cit.,* 172–208 (188), but see also 108 and 161

38 M. Herzfeld, *Anthropology through the Looking Glass: Critical Ethnology in the Margins of Europe,* Cambridge: Cambridge University Press 1987, 9–21

39 H.C. Prince, 'Modernization, restoration, preservation: changes in taste for antique landscapes', In: A.R.H. Baker and M. Billinge (eds.), *Period and Place: Research Methods in Historical Geography,* Cambridge: Cambridge University Press, 1982, 33–40

40 B.M. Silvestro, *Western European Travellers to Mainland Greece, 1700–1800,* Ph.D. Thesis, University of Wisconsin, 1959, 355

41 L. Logan, 'The geographical imagination of Frederic Remington: the inventor of the Cowboy West', *Journal of Historical Geography,* 18 (1987), 75–90

journeys, they draw together material about particular topics in a systematic and thoughtful way. Thus, in the third volume of his *Voyage en Grèce*, the Sicilian economist and Director of Agriculture and Commerce for the Venetian Republic, Xavier Scrofani, suddenly abandoned the letter format which he had adopted to describe his antiquarian travels in Greece (1794–95) and embarked upon a systematic discussion of the agriculture and trade of the Morea, complete with tables of the imports and exports[42]. Incidentally, these statistics have been accepted uncritically, at least partly because they are available[43]. The French Consul in Salonica at the same date was Felix de Beaujour[44]. He published a series of letters, allegedly written while travelling in the 1790s, which describe aspects of the economy of various parts of Greece and include one of the earliest published accounts of the famous textile town of Ambelakia in eastern Thessaly[45]. The sources used by both Beaujour and Scrofani are unclear.

The late Steven Runciman observed in his book on Mistra that 'for the eighteenth century and early nineteenth the most valuable information comes from the accounts of Western travellers'[46]. Twenty years on such an assertion cannot go unchallenged. There is at least an obligation on the scholar to use whatever locally produced sources may be available. Leake himself owned and drew upon the geographies of Bishop Meletius and Father Daniel Philippedes, published respectively in Venice (1728) and Vienna (1791)[47]. Eighteenth century sources available to us now include letters and journals; family papers such as wills, marriage settlements and leases; court decisions; and administrative documents such as tax surveys. All too often these rich sources have simply been avoided. The reasons are straightforward. They have not always been easy to find. Ability in Greek, the Venetian dialect of Italian and Ottoman Turkish are required, as well as skills in palaeography and diplomatic. However, a once gloomy situation has improved. Access to archives is now easier for scholars. Catalogues are fuller and some published editions of documents are available[48]. Linguistic and related skills are still limited, but the emergence of a tradition of multi-disciplinary, communal scholarship is overcoming the limitations of the lone scholar. Importantly, the experts themselves are now finding the eighteenth century an attractive period for research after the long dominance of the so-called classical period amongst

42 X. Scrofani, *Voyage en Grece de Xavier Scrofani, Sicilien, fait en 1794 et 1795*, Paris 1801; Silvestro, *op. cit.*, 1959, 58–59

43 Β. Κρεμμυδᾶς, *Συγκύρια καί Εμπόριο στὴν Προεπαναστάτικη Πελοπόννησο (1793–1821)*, Athens: Themelio, 1980

44 Silvestro. *op. cit.*, 63–64

45 Felix de Beaujour *Tableau du Commerce de la Grèce, formé d'aprés une année moyenne depuis 1787 jusqu'a 1797*, Paris 1800, pp. 272–85, 290–91

46 S. Runciman, *Mistra: Byzantine Capital of the Peloponnese*, London: Thames and Hudson, 1980, 152

47 Meletios, *Γεωγραφία Παλαιά καί Νέα ...*, Venice 1728 [Leake's edition 1807]; D. Philippedes, *Η Γεωγραφία Νεωτερίκη*, 1791; W. Martin Leake, '. . . *A Catalogue of Books, Having reference to My Collection of Coins and Antiquities . . ., 1858'*, University of Cambridge: Institute of Classical Studies Library

48 Faroqui, *op. cit.*

Ottomanists and Byzantium or the War of Independence among the Hellenes. When thinking of documentary sources, though, it is worth remembering, that with the exception of the area of Selanik (Thessaloniki or Salonica), most of the territory of what is now Greece was not in the core of the Ottoman Empire. Parts of it had high strategic significance in Ottoman relations with Western Europe and some economic value, but Greece as a whole was on the periphery and of limited importance. Moreover, Greece was contested space for at least a hundred years, from the sporadic uprisings of 1821 to the wars of expansion and liberation in the late nineteenth and early twentieth centuries. For both reasons, the expected Greek and Turkish documentation is not always there. By contrast, Venetian sources for Crete, the Morea and the Ionian Islands are surprisingly rich, especially for geographers because they include not only maps and plans, but also accounts which refer to weather.

Greater use of Greek, Ottoman and Venetian sources will enrich the study of the historical geography of Greece in the 'long' eighteenth century. Comparative studies have already begun to provide an essential check on the data presented by many of the travellers and this could be taken further[49]. Without access to relevant Greek or Turkish documents, it has proved difficult to assess the validity of the non-observational material which the historical geographer might wish to use. The early travellers seldom reveal the sources of their socio-economic information.

There are other problems, too. The non-observational material presented by the travellers has been mediated in various ways. First, the published text was the result of a process of selection and editing in a context dominated by classical learning but where the eighteenth century reader expected some socio-economic content, and where we recognise, under the influence of post-modernism, that knowledge is both ideologically and socially constructed[50]. Second, many of the travellers had little or no serviceable Greek, let alone Albanian, Turkish or Vlach. The non-observational material they present was sometimes obtained from consuls, western merchants and physicians resident in Greece. Out in the field, it must have been mediated through the *dragoman*. He was part interpreter, part guide and part 'Mr Fix-it'. Such people were often engaged in the Ionian Islands and shared a third language with their employer, usually Italian. The *dragoman* relayed the information provided by hosts, guides, escorts, merchants and officials (lay and ecclesiastical) in response to the traveller's questions, probably in abbreviated and distorted form. Possibly the *dragoman* translated documents provided for the earnest traveller.

For the modern scholar using such problematic sources as travel narratives it is imperative, as Lovell observed[51], that the interpretation of the sources is as tight,

49 Bennet, Davis and Zarinebaf-Shahr, *op. cit.*; M. Kiel and F. Sauerwein, *Ost Lokris in türkischer und neogriechischer Zeit (1460–1981)*, Passau: Passavia Üniversitatsverlag, 1994, 46–57

50 M. Domosh, 'Towards a feminist historiography of geography', *Transactions of the Institute of British Geographers*, ns 16 (1991), 95–104

51 W.G. Lovell, 'Mayans, missionaries, evidence and truth: the polemics of native re-settlement in sixteenth century Guatemala', *Journal of Historical Geography*, 16 (1990), 277–94

creative and contextualised as possible, and that ambiguities, contradictions, divergences and incompleteness are recognised and rigorously dealt with. Reviews in such contemporary periodicals as *The Gentleman's Magazine* and the *Edinburgh Review* provide some help. In the early nineteenth century particularly, the potential audience was concerned with 'accuracy', as well as liveliness of style, and the better reviewers recognised the 'situated' nature of the accounts they were reading[52]. Otherwise, we are obliged to apply the usual principles of historical criticism to the travel narratives: internal consistency, opportunity to observe or collect what is reported, comparison with other travel narratives, and evidence of bias and exaggeration. The quality of the traveller as an observer and reporter can also be evaluated. One approach to this draws upon the techniques of content analysis (Figure 1)[53].

The traveller produced a *record* of the journey. This may survive as a manuscript journal or a set of letters, as well as the published book. The *record* itself results from the *observations* made by the traveller, but includes socio-economic material collected from third parties. Differences between the manuscript journal, written in the field, and the published version reveal much about the editorial process. What the traveller saw and recorded was affected by his/her *viewpoint*. That, in turn, was conditioned by the route followed, by the comfort of the journey and access to information. The traveller's comfort was affected by the *materiality* of the journey: the availability and quality of horses, the condition of the roads, the quality of accommodation, and the state of the weather. Also important were the incidence of personal illness and the risk of attack by disease and bandits. Access to socio-economic data required conversation with potential informants. The ability to talk directly to them depended upon the languages spoken by the traveller. Linguistic competence affected the degree of dependence upon the *dragoman*. Language ability, in turn, was conditioned by background and education. These, of course, shaped the ideas and expectations which the traveller took out with him/her – ' the pre-encounter lore', in Wright's phrase[54]. Contemporary attitudes to education and different cultures created filters. Education and background frequently provided the reasons for the journey to Greece in the first place and then determined the places chosen for a visit. Access to the chosen places was shaped by their relative location with respect to the ports or other entry points. The spatial relationships then conditioned the routes followed. Given a dominant interest in Antiquity, as mediated by a selective reading of Greek and Latin authors, it is hardly surprising that travellers in the 'long' eighteenth century tended to visit the same places and that their itineraries are very similar. Chance, however, also had an effect. For example, gales took

52 W.C. Brown, 'Byron and English interest in the Near East', *Studies in Philology*, 34 (1937), 55–64

53 K. Krippendorff, *Content Analysis: An Introduction*, Beverly Hills and London: Sage 1980

54 J.K. Wright, *Human Nature in Geography. Fourteen Papers, 1925–1965*, Cambridge: Cambridge University Press 1966

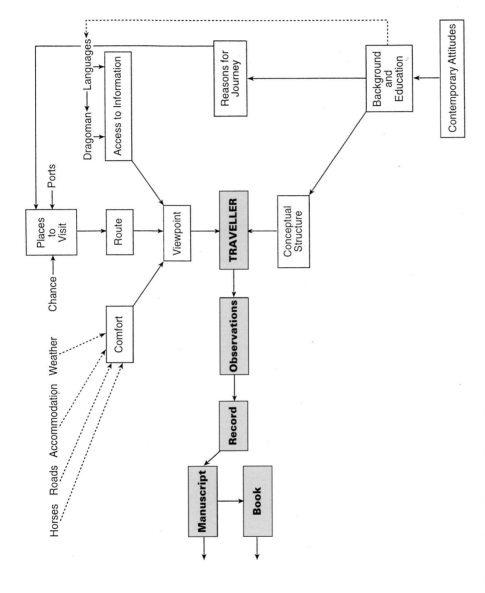

FIGURE 1 Scheme for Evaluating a Travel Narrative

some travellers to an unexpected port and that accident conditioned at least the early part of their journeys. François Pouqueville was unlucky enough to be taken by privateers, but capture deposited him in the Morea; his experiences and conversations provided the material for his account of the region[55].

Examination of each element in this analytical model provides material for evaluating the qualities and opportunities of the traveller as an observer and recorder. Indirectly, the process allows the reliability of the resulting narrative to be tested. Lack of evaluation has been the greatest weakness in the use of travel narratives for the sorts of historico-geographical purposes which I indicated earlier, especially those for which 'hard' information is required.

I conclude, then, with a note of caution. Before early travel narratives are used for studies in the historical geography of Greece, source criticism is required. The texts themselves must be read carefully and not simply plundered for their data. They must be understood in the context of their times and as examples of a particular literary genre. Certain general rules governed their composition. The target audience often knew, or thought it knew, a good deal about Greece already and had certain expectations of each new travel book[56]. A certain socio-economic content was part of that, but so too were incident, colour, and ancient ruins. The limitations of each travel narrative must be appreciated, rather than blanked out with some bland statement. Travel narratives are available, attractive and potentially useful sources. These qualities, however, should not deflect us from the fundamental scholarly work which, I am sure, John Myres would have advocated.

55 F.C.H.L. Pouqueville, *Voyage en Morée à Constantinople, et en Albanie . . . pendant les Années 1798, 1799, 1800 et 1801*, Paris 1805

56 T. Spencer, *Fair Greece Sad Relic*, London: Weidenfeld and Nicolson, 1954

J. L. MYRES MEMORIAL LECTURES

I	1961	Professor B. Ashmole	Forgeries of Ancient Sculpture, Creation and Detection
II	1963	J. B. Ward Perkins	Landscape and History in Central Italy
III	1965	Professor F. W. Walbank	Speeches in Greek Historians
IV	1967	Lieut. Gen. Sir John Glubb	The Mixture of Races in the Eastern Arab Countries
V★	1970	Professor C. F. A. Schaeffer	John L. Myres and Cyprus Archaeology
VI	1971	Professor W. G. East	The Destruction of Cities in the Mediterranean World
VII	1973	Professor A. D. Momigliano	Polybius between the English and the Turks
VII	1975	Professor C. F. C. Hawkes	Pytheas: Europe and the Greek Explorers
IX★	1977	Dr J. K. Campbell	Heroes and Disorder in the Greek Tradition
X	1979	Dr J. N. L. Myres	Commander J. L. Myres, R.N.V.R.: The Blackbeard of the Aegean
XI	1981	Professor A. M. Snodgrass	Narration and Allusion in Archaic Greek Art
XII	1983	Professor I. J. Gottmann	Orbits: The Ancient Mediterranean Tradition of Urban Networks
XII	1985	Dr V. Karageorghis	The Archaeology of Cyprus: The Ninety Years after Myres
XIV	1987	Dr H. W. Catling	Some Problems in Aegean Prehistory c.1450–1380 B.C.
XV	1989	Professor J. P. A. Gould	Give and Take in Herodotus
XVI	1991	Professor C. Nicolet	Financial Documents and Geographical Knowledge in the Roman World
XVII	1993	Professor Sir John Boardman	Classical Art in Eastern Translation
XVIII★	1995	Professor A. M. Davies	Dialect, History and Prehistory in Ancient Greece
XIX	1997	Professor J. N. Coldstream	Light from Cyprus on the Greek 'Dark Age'
XX	1999	Professor O. Rackham	Trees, Wood, and Timber in Greek History
XXI	2001	Amélie Kuhrt	'Greeks' and 'Greece' in Mesopotamian and Persian Perspectives

★ *Not Published*